Stopwatch books in hardback

Apple tree	Ladybird
Butterfly and caterpillar	Mosquito
Chicken and egg	Moth
Conker	Mushroom
Dandelion	Newt
Dragonfly	Potato
Earwig	Stickleback
Fly	Strawberry
Honeybee	Tadpole and frog
House mouse	Tomato

First paperback edition 1991
Reprinted 1992

First published 1985 by
Forlaget Apostrof, Copenhagen, Denmark
Published in 1985 in hardback by
A & C Black (Publishers) Limited
35 Bedford Row, London WC1R 4JH

ISBN 0–7136–3498–7

A CIP catalogue record for this book
is available from the British Library.

Acknowledgements
The artwork is by B L Kearley Ltd
Photographs: pg 5, G1 Bernard/Oxford Scientific Films; pg 10, Zoologisk Museum,
Copenhagen; pg 16, Hands Lind.
The publishers would like to thank Jean Imrie for her help and advice.

Filmset by August Filmsetting, Haydock, St Helens
Printed in Belgium by Proost International Book Production

Snail

Jens Olesen
Photography by Bo Jarner

A & C Black · London

Here is a snail.

Have you ever touched a snail?

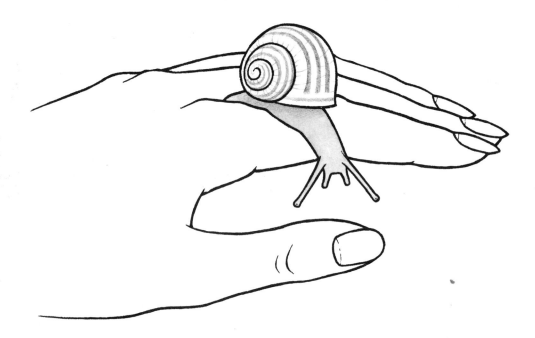

The snail has a hard shell but its body is soft and slimy. Snails need to keep their bodies damp. If their bodies dry up, the snails will die. So they hide under stones or in dark damp places.

This book will tell you about snails.

In winter the snail hides and sleeps.
The snail wakes up in spring.

When winter comes, the snail burrows into the ground.
Then it goes inside its shell, like this.

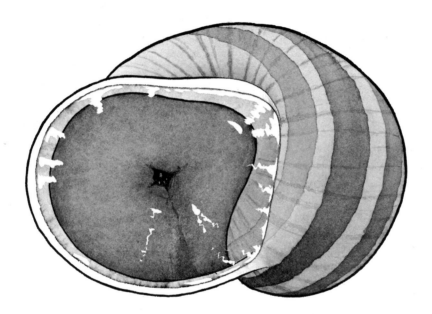

Can you see the entrance to the shell? The snail
covers the entrance with a layer of slime. Soon the
slime goes hard. The snail is safe inside its shell.
It will stay there all winter.

Look at the photograph. On a warm rainy day in spring,
the snail wakes up.

The snail glides along on its foot.

The snail has a long flat foot to help it move.
Look at the big photograph. You can see the foot
from underneath.

The foot squashes up at the back and stretches out
at the front. This is how the snail creeps forward.

The snail makes a layer of slime under its foot.
This helps it to glide along. The slime also protects
the snail's foot. The snail can crawl over a sharp stone
or a piece of glass. Its foot will not get scratched.

The snail looks for food.

Look at the big picture. The snail is searching for
food. Can you see the feelers on the snail's head?
There are two short feelers and two long feelers.
The short feelers are for touching and tasting.

Here is a close-up picture of the long feelers.

Can you see the dot on the end of each feeler?
The dots are eyes. The snail cannot see very well.
But it can tell the difference between light and dark.

The snail eats plants.

Look at the big photograph. It shows the snail's head from underneath. Can you see a tiny hole just below the feelers? This is the snail's mouth.

The snail has a flat tongue which is covered with tiny spikes. This picture shows the spikes very large.

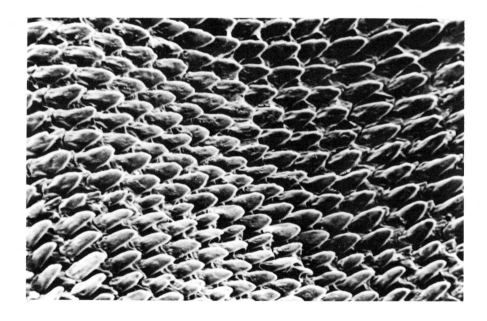

The snail rubs its tongue against a leaf. The tongue works rather like a cheese grater. It scrapes off small pieces of leaf for the snail to eat.

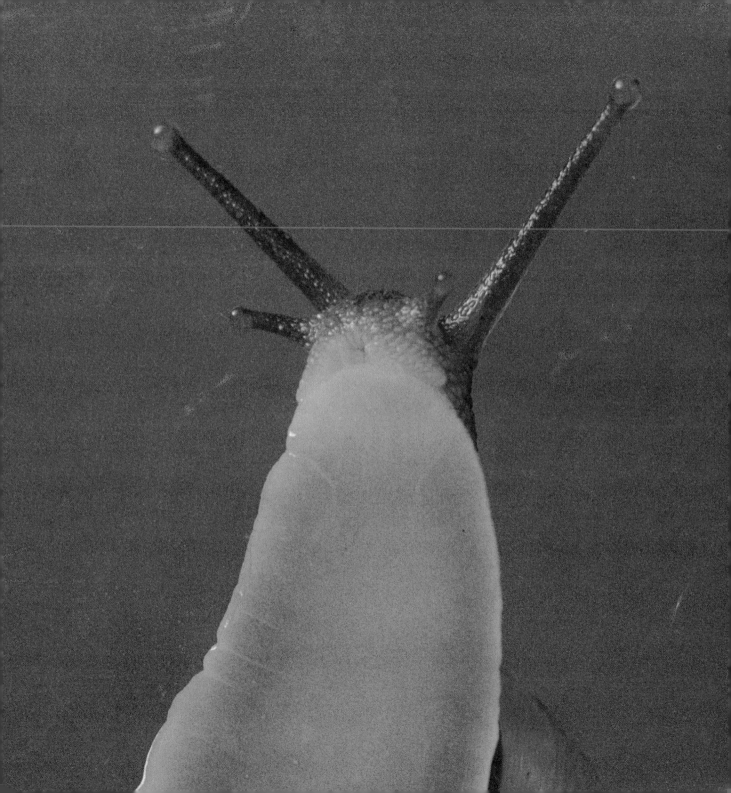

The snail has a hard shell.

If the snail is frightened, it goes inside its shell.
This helps to keep the snail safe from enemies.

Lots of animals like to eat snails. This bird smashes
the snail's shell against a rock. Then it eats the
snail's soft body.

There are many kinds of snails. They all have shells
to hide in. Look at all the different snail shells in
the photograph.

The snail breathes through a hole in its shell.

When the snail feels safe it comes out of its shell.
The snail puts its head out. Then its feelers unfold.

Look at the photograph. Can you see a hole in the
snail's shell? The snail breathes in and out through
this hole. It has lungs and breathes air like we do.

The snail finds a mate.

When the weather gets warmer, the snail looks for
a mate. Look at the photograph. These two snails are
going to mate.

Each snail shoots a tiny dart into the body of its
mate. This picture shows the darts very large.

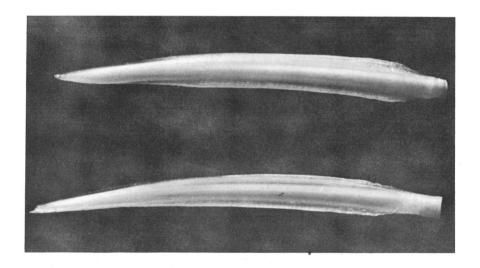

The snails swap darts.
Then they mate with each other.

The snails lay eggs.

A few weeks after they have mated, the snails lay eggs.
Both the snails can lay eggs.

Look at the big photograph. This snail is laying its eggs
in the ground. It covers the eggs with earth and then
it goes away. The snail will never see its eggs again.

Because the snail has mated, the eggs start to develop.
Inside each egg, a tiny snail begins to grow.

Can you see the snail shells growing inside the eggs?

Tiny snails come out of the eggs.

After four weeks, the eggs are ready to hatch.
Look at the big photograph. The egg shells split open
and the tiny snails crawl out.

The young snails look like their parents but they are
much smaller. Their shells are soft and thin.

The snails are hungry. First they eat the empty
eggshells. Then they look for young plants to eat.

Slowly the snails grow bigger.

Look at the big photograph. This snail is only a few weeks old. You can almost see through its shell.

Soon the snail's shell will go hard and change colour. By the end of the summer, the snail will have a stripy shell like its parents.

The snail will live and grow for three years. Next spring, the snail will be ready to mate and lay eggs.

What do you think will happen to the eggs?

Do you remember how a snail is born and grows up?
See if you can tell the story in your own words.
You can use these pictures to help you.

Index

This index will help you to find some of the important words in the book

Try making a snail garden. Put some stones and damp earth in an old fish tank. Keep a cover (with small holes in) over the tank. Don't forget to keep the earth damp and put fresh leaves in the tank every day. When you have finished watching them, put the snails back where they came from.